DAVE
and the STORKS

Written by

Jenny Phillips

Illustrated by

Ekaterina Kolesnikova

Challenge Words

blue

out

spider

stork

CHAPTER 1

Dave Sanchez got up. Robins flapped by him and landed on a branch. Dave looked at them.

A robin dropped mud on the branch.

"What is the robin doing?" Dave asked Mom.

"Oh, it will be a nest!"
Mom said.

A robin left. Then it was

back with mud. It left. Then it was back with grass and twigs.

Dave had his mush. Then he dashed out to see the robins.

He was still and looked up. The robins had sticks and moss.

Dave looked to his left and jumped back. A big black thing was on a web.

It was a spider. Dave did not love that spider, so he left that spot.

The next day, Dave
helped Dad cut the grass.
As they passed the web,

Dave looked at the spider.
No, he did not love it. No,
not at all.

In three days the robin
had a nest of mud, moss,
twigs, and grass.

"Will it lay eggs?" Dave asked his mom. Mom hugged Dave. "Yes, it will. This is so fun for us to see."

That day, Dave played and played. But he did not go by the spider.

His ball went by the
spider, so Dave just left his
ball there.

The next day, Dave got
up and looked at the nest.
"An egg!" he said.
It was blue.

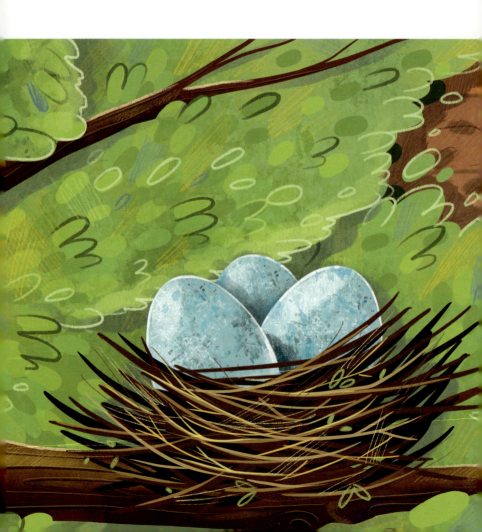

By the end of the week, three eggs sat in the nest. They had black specks on them.

CHAPTER 2

It was still spring. The robin sat on its nest. The ball still sat by the spider.

Dave looked up. Two
storks sat on the bricks.
They had twigs.

Dave dashed to Mom.

"A stork nest!" he said.

"There will be a stork nest

up there!"

It was fun to see the

storks with branches.

Three days passed. Then the storks sat in the nest.

Dave loved spring.

He did this.

He did that.

He did this.

But he did NOT get his ball.

"I do not love that black spider," he said.

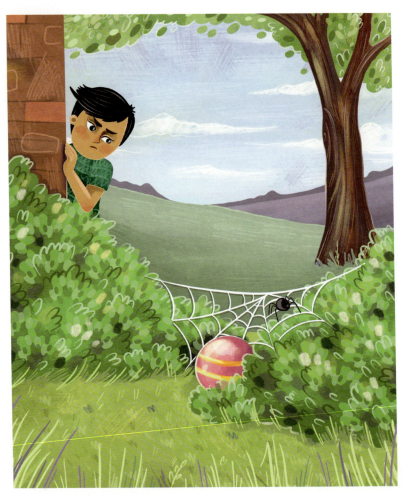

But Dave did love the storks. "There must be eggs in the nest," he said.

CHAPTER 3

One day, Dave got up. He looked at the robin nest.

"OOOOOooohhhhhhh!"

One of the eggs was cracking.

It was not until the end of the day that the chick got out of the egg.

By the end of three days, all three chicks had gotten out of the eggs.

They did not have fluff.

"This is the way they look for a bit," Mom said.

The mom
and dad
robins helped
the chicks.

All day, the dad robin fed
the chicks.

All day, the mom robin
fed the chicks.

It was not long until Dave looked up and spotted stork chicks.

Three chicks peeked out
from the big nest.

Dave loved to see the robin chicks and the stork chicks.

This is what the robin chicks had for lunch:

 moths

crickets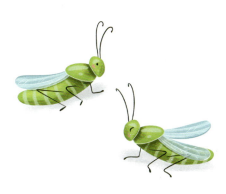

 ants

But still, he did not love to
see the spider. He stayed
a long way from it.

This is what the stork chicks had for lunch:

 fish

frogs

 grubs

This is what Dave had for lunch. Yum!

Dave was glad he was not a robin or a stork. Yes,

Dave was glad that his
lunch was not grubs and
moths.

At the end of the day,
Dave was snug in bed. But

then the wind picked up,
and there was a flash!

It was so wet. The wind bent the trees. The sky flashed and flashed.

"Oh no!" Dave said. "The storks! The robins!"

The next day,
the sun was up.
The land was
wet, but the day
was still.

Dave dashed out. The stork and robin chicks peeked out of the nests. "Yay!" Dave called.

Then a stork swooped to the web and grabbed the black spider.

"YAY!" called Dave as he got the ball. "I love having storks and robins!"